ALLEGHENY, BC

Allegheny, BC

Rodney DeCroo

Nightwood Editions
2012

Nightwood Editions
P.O. Box 1779
Gibsons, BC VON 1VO
Canada
www.nightwoodeditions.com

Nightwood Editions acknowledges financial support from the Government of
Canada through the Canada Book Fund and the Canada Council for the Arts, and
from the Province of British Columbia through the British Columbia Arts Council
and the Book Publisher's Tax Credit.

This book has been produced on 100% post-consumer recycled, ancient-forest-free
paper, processed chlorine-free and printed with vegetable-based dyes.

TYPESETTING & COVER DESIGN: Carleton Wilson
COVER PHOTOGRAPH: Brad Yaksich

Printed and bound in Canada

LIBRARY AND ARCHIVES CANADA CATALOGUING IN PUBLICATION

DeCroo, Rodney, 1966-
Allegheny, BC / Rodney DeCroo.

ISBN 978-0-88971-274-4

1. DeCroo, Rodney, 1966- --Poetry. I. Title.

PS8557.E255A45 2012   C811'.6   C2012-903630-7

CONTENTS

I

11   On the Night of My First Breath

13   The Allegheny

15   Winter

16   The Path

18   Fishing

19   The Widow

20   Rock Fight

22   The Tire Garage

24   *Pittsburgh Post-Gazette*

25   Colfax Street

26   The Russian Painter of Pittsburgh

28   Poplar Trees

II

31   Five Years Old

32   The Wrecked Farm (Indiana County, Pennsylvania)

34   Cherry Valley, Pennsylvania

36   Oil Drum

38   Dayspring Christian Academy

39   Mr. Steigel

42   Mother (Northern British Columbia)

43   Gary Powell's Outfitters

46   Heart Lake

51   Trumpeter Swan

III

55 The Hunting Knife
56 The Lightning Catcher
58 Mining for Gold
60 Pink Mountain
62 Mrs. Tobin
68 Fight
70 Everywhere You Look
72 My Father's Watch

IV

75 Starlings
76 Willy Soble
78 The Ride
80 The Song That Says
81 Home
82 The Trumpet
83 What Is Ours
84 Days Like This
86 Behind the Gasworks on Railroad Avenue
88 Ruins
89 Certain Things
90 Marked

93 Acknowledgements
95 About the Author

I

On the Night of My First Breath

On the night of my first breath in a delivery room
at Allegheny County General Hospital, my birth father
whom I will never meet is asleep on a bus

disappearing into the Midwest. His name is Frank
Houser. His jacket is crumpled between the side
of his face and the window. It is the 29th

of December, but he dreams rain coming down
so hard, long strands strike the glass as if to shatter it.
My father's hands are twitching in his lap

and when he looks down a sparrow is nesting
as if in the crook of a tree. Warmth like joy
fills my father's body because

so delicate a creature has chosen him for safety.
He lightly strokes the small brown head
with the tip of a finger. The bird begins singing

into the darkness of the bus. Its high, sweet trilling
travels among the sleeping passengers,
drawing each breath into its praise. My father

knows he is as much this song
as anything else in his life. When he looks outside
the rain has subsided into a blazing mist

lit red by the furnaces of steel mills along the river.
Upwards through the mist, against the darkness,
black smoke rises over the city like the sparrow's notes

rising through my father's hands into the night
of this place he is leaving. When he looks down again
his lap is empty. A woman nudges him awake

as the bus pulls into the Cleveland terminal.
Piles of plowed snow are crusted black
beneath the white lights of the empty parking lot.

He stares out the window, trying to remember
what he was dreaming. He is asked if he is getting off here
and he says no, he has much farther to go.

The Allegheny

What a filthy river! Lined with steel mills
and factories, to swim in it was to smell
for days the oily stink against your skin,
a nausea-twist in your stomach,

uneasy reminder of the river's phlegmy,
dark green clutch. It was as dangerous
as it was dirty. The bottom dug out
for gravel, unnaturally and unevenly deep,

held invisible currents, eddies, undertows
that could pull, suck and hold you down
until you drowned, or throw you up again
to limb-flash, flail and suck for air.

Each summer it claimed a child
from the cancerous towns along its sides,
as if it were an angry, wounded god
demanding tribute. Each summer

we gathered there to fish for monstrous carp
and catfish no one would ever eat, to swim
and dunk each other beneath the blinding water,
to watch the rich kids carve into the current

white-tipped waves, bronzed bodies balanced
on single skis behind small, sleek powerboats.
By the docks we bobbed in water warm as blood,
the sunlight marching like fire across the oily surface

to burn away all but summer's touch.
We swam beside the hulk of coal barges
black as the bible's curse that tore the earth.
All summer we swam in it. What a filthy river!

Winter

The river's jammed along its sides
with slabs of ice all crumpled
against each other like car wrecks.
The sun is a moth against the blue.

Cold light on the white ground.
It will soon be as dark as the slim,
open channel of black water that runs
through the centre of the ice pack.

I'm standing on the shore,
my fingers stiff as I toss
lit matches to burn out
in the snow. I pretend the river ice

is set to explode with each spark,
but there's no sound, only
the blackened stems lying around
my boots like burnt fingernails.

The Path

Behind the Super Dollar Grocery
a footpath cuts along the embankment
down to the tracks, the woods and the river.

A strip of dust and crushed grass,
it leads to forgotten factories,
weeds, broken glass, truant children

and vagrants who roam the scrub woods
that hide the river from the town.
My two brothers and I take it

at a stooping run until we cross the tracks
to slip unseen into the shadowed light
amongst the trees. The path weaves

between the slender poplar trunks
and tangled brush until it reaches
the water's edge. Here, we sit in the sun

on a ruined concrete slab and watch
the river moving past us. The cement
is warm and rough against our bare legs

and the palms of our hands. Across
the river a tugboat silently pushes three
coal barges downstream. The small,

dark shapes of men on the decks
of the tug are distorted by the heat waves
above the water. They waver and shimmer

and blink out. Coal piles are mountains
of blackened ashes atop barges
dragging the deep and murky current.

My brother Lynn breaks the stupor we're
in because of the heat, wondering out loud
who made the path that we just took.

Fishing

The remains of a bridge, giant slabs
of concrete, lie in jumbled piles along
the riverbank. Underneath, in crevices,
huge river rats search for their food—
the fleshly grey and swollen shapes

of dead carp and catfish that float
up from the Allegheny River's depths
to rot in a wash of yellowish scum.
Sometimes my brothers and I, seated
on our concrete perches, see a flash

of brown, hear a slap of body entering
water, or find a half-eaten fish bloated
in the sunlight. And although we're boys,
we don't speak of rats or the chewed-
on flesh kicked back into the dark.

We mould dough balls around barbed
hooks and attach leaden sinkers to our lines.
We stand, slowly swing our rods behind us,
then in one quick, forward motion cast
our baited hooks out into the river.

The Widow

Mrs. O'Donnell lived next door
to my grandparents on Pillow Avenue.
No one went into her yard or the woods
behind her place. She was a widow—
her husband crushed by a coal car.

After he died she disappeared
into her house and was seldom seen
in town. Mr. Podmilsak
delivered groceries to her every week,
and according to my grandma,

went to the liquor store on her behalf.
When Uncle Robert died in the mine
my grandma found a wreath
outside their door with a letter
from Mrs. O'Donnell. After that

the rumours stopped coming out
of my grandma's mouth. Neither
would she hear them spread by anyone else.
Leave the woman alone, she'd say.
No one has a right to judge.

Rock Fight

Running between stacks
of concrete blocks we'd throw rocks
at each other. We used small stones
hardly bigger than pebbles

and aimed for the legs or back.
If you got hit you were dead. The war
was won by the last man standing
and then we'd start all over again.

Sometimes it was each man
for himself or we'd play by teams.
I'd hide at the edge of a stack,
wait for someone to run

past and hit them from behind.
Once, as I was watching, I heard
a noise and turned around. A stone
struck my head and knocked me

down. For a moment there was
only the sharp white light
and the pain of the blow. Billy
and my brothers were standing

above me. Chris clutched a stone
in his hand. Lynn knelt down,
took off his shirt and pressed it
to the side of my head. Billy

kept saying, *I didn't mean to Rod,*
I didn't mean to Rod, until Chris
gently patted his shoulder.
I held my hand to my face

and when I brought it back
to look, it was bright with blood,
but not nearly as bright
as the circle we made.

The Tire Garage

When I was ten years old we lived
above a tire garage set in an alley.
Mornings, as my brothers and I

readied for school, below us
the racket sounded: the clank of tools
against concrete, buzzing air guns

loosening lug nuts, and men
shouting while they worked.
Occasionally, through the linoleum-

covered floorboards, as we
ate breakfast or brushed our teeth,
a word or phrase would float

up as clear and close
as if we had spoken it.
Sometimes *Fuck!* or *Shit!*

or *Jesus Christ!*—my mother's
face hardening as we grinned.
Sometimes a name *Larry*

or *Greg* or an object: *crowbar*
or *generator*. Sometimes a command:
Get the phone! or *Shut up!*

My mother would play cassettes
to mask the noise from below
with the frenzied shouts of evangelists.

But God's apocalyptic word blaring
from my mother's tape deck
was never as thrilling to me

as the voices sounding
their toiling speech
into the living air among us.

Pittsburgh Post-Gazette

You slump down the stairs wrapped
in a parka and several layers of clothing.
You wish you were lying in the blanket's
oven not going out into this ice-age
morning to deliver the *Post-Gazette*

to widows and retired miners. They irritate
you as they sit in their kitchens at 5 a.m.
to watch for you through frozen windows.
There's a half-hour to sleep if you finish
early, but you have to stand on porches

to wait for them to fumble open doors.
The women ask if you are cold and need
to warm yourself a moment. They lightly
touch your arm and offer food or a cup
of tea. The old men gruffly call you

back to press a dime or quarter tip
into your glove. Sometimes they place
a hand upon your shoulder before you
turn to step back down the stairs into
the morning's darkness and the crush

of snow beneath your boots. The ink-blackened
canvas bag bangs off your thigh as you
move from house to house in the silence.
You wish that you were invisible—while those
who watch you wish that they were seen.

Colfax Street

I stand outside an apartment
building and stare at a lit window
three storeys above me. A woman
is moving around a room.

I can make out her shape,
a soft darkness against
the backdrop of the light.
I'm reminded of the inky form

of an embryo I saw pulsing
in a glowing egg at school but I'm
not in a classroom. I'm standing
on Colfax Street in the freezing darkness

for the third night in a row,
watching a woman I don't know
while she prepares for sleep.
I look down at my grey sneakers

and finger the Goodwill jacket
on my back, and know,
for the first time, how much
I hate this place.

The Russian Painter of Pittsburgh

He painted Russian religious icons
for a living, though whom he sold them
to wasn't clear. People said he lived
off his mother's pension. They lived
in a small brick house on Pillow Avenue.
What was more important: he was
a Russian and therefore a Communist.
An ignorant supposition, yes, but this
was working-class Pittsburgh in the early
eighties at the height of the Cold War.
He wore a threadbare black overcoat
the colour of his straggling long hair
and smoked cigarettes that stained
his long delicate fingers. His eyes
flamed a fierce bright blue. You could
often see him walking the streets
staring up at the chestnut trees,
the huge pockets of his overcoat
bulging with green chestnuts he collected
from the sidewalks and gutters.

One winter Sunday he stood
outside the local movie theatre
after the matinee had ended
giving out his paintings:

chestnut trees consumed in fire, ringed
by the faces of Russian saints
on small, unframed oil canvases
that he thrust into people's hands.

Poplar Trees

The fall, that's what stays with me;
there was nothing like the fall in Pennsylvania.
After school I'd rush home to the farm to get
my shotgun and go straight into the fields

and the woods. I'd hunt the stubbled corn
fields first, try to flush out doves or a grouse
or maybe a rabbit. Often I wouldn't see
anything but sparrows in the trees

by the tractor path. So I'd go into the woods.
It was quiet there and the trees made
the quiet move inside you the way
the branches moved inside the wind

without a sound. A different hunting
started then. I'd wade through oak leaves
like fossil imprints of prehistoric fish
millions of years old, but it's the poplar

trees I remember most. Slender, pale girls
reaching up into the upside-down
blue waters of the sky, thousands of gold
and red eyes glittering above me.

II

Five Years Old

The linoleum is cold beneath your feet,
the moonlight dumps frigid ashes

on the kitchen counters, the windows
are black like the TV's dead face,

and your heart thumping
in your chest like a small landed fish

gives you away to the silence
oozing from the furniture, walls and ceiling

when the front door swings open,
and the light and drunken laughter is like a slap,

and you see you mother's smeared face, her
returning eyes like abandoned nests.

The Wrecked Farm (Indiana County, Pennsylvania)

The highway is a mile from the house,
but at night I hear the cars and pretend
it's the sound of breakers on a distant shore,

knowing there's no ocean for four hundred
miles, just farms, roads, woods. I whisper
into the room, *The river is a body*

that carries your dreams. Its currents
are the words trapped in your hands—
words I wrote on a piece of paper

I burned at the back of the barn,
afraid someone might see what I did.
It was quiet. Not even a crow croaking

from the copse of rotted poplars,
only black smoke curling upwards
into a manic cloud of gnats, the pasture

dying with the summer, the barn planks
collapsing like a toothless old face.
I hated that place. My uncle's huge,

scarred hands wielding his greasy bible,
my aunt's thin, feral-cat face.
Clinging to their wrecked farm

like ghosts jealous of the living,
except for church or groceries
they seldom left that desiccated ground.

Cherry Valley, Pennsylvania

It was a two-hour drive to Mr. Stahura's
Christmas tree farm in Cherry Valley—
several hundred acres of squat pines
planted in orderly rows along the hills.

My grandfather and I made the trip
in his old Chevy truck, rifles
tied to the rack behind our heads
to hunt for white-tailed deer. It was

late December and the woods
and fields were deep with snow.
I climbed up a ladder of two-by-fours
to a rough stand of planks

all nailed to an old oak tree.
My grandfather handed up the rifles
and our packs, then climbed the ladder
to join me. We sat side by side watching

the snowed-in field of shrouded trees
for any movement. The countryside
was one vast moment of continuous
silence. My grandfather

placed his gloved hand on my knee
and nodded toward my left. I slowly
turned my head and saw a herd
of six does and two bucks

stepping lightly into the clearing
just beneath our tree. They'd
come from the wooded gully
behind us and were heading

toward the half-empty field
of planted pines, but now
they were stopped, gathered
in a loose bunch, the bucks

leading to scout the path, ears peaked
to catch the slightest sound, black nostrils
quivering to detect scents on the air,
as the does dipped their heads

to look for the odd dried stalk
to feed upon. I slipped the safety
with my thumb and slowly stood,
raising the rifle to my shoulder

to sight the largest buck
in the crosshairs of my scope.
I aimed for the heart,
and squeezed the trigger.

Oil Drum

We throw balled-up sheets of newspaper,
dead twigs and branches into a rusted
oil drum. We light several matches and toss
them inside. The paper catches fire and soon
flames are crackling and our shadows

begin to loom and waver against the trees
and the river. We pass around stolen cans
of beer and pop the tabs and laugh as foam
spills over our hands and onto our sneakers.
My brother Chris asks if I like the taste of beer.

Fuckin' right I do! but the truth is I hate it.
Doesn't matter because I've already
begun at thirteen to need it. We talk about
girls and lie about the things we've done
with them. I count each can and wonder

how many more I'll need for later that night
when we go to the Ches-A-Rena to roller
skate and watch the girls we've been lying
about. We talk about our friend Denny
sent away to Shuman Centre for burning

down the building where he lived
with his mother and sister who drink
more than most men and fight almost as hard.
Once they attacked two girls twirling batons
in the middle of the July 4th parade because

the sister said they'd called her a whore
at school. Jeff jokes and says some big
mutant's probably nailing Denny's ass
as we speak, but it's not funny because
Lester's going to youth court next week

for stealing a handgun. He might be
sent away just like any one of us could
be the way things happen so fast. We're
all quiet as we stare down into the oil
drum at the flames that leap into the air

as if trying to fly back to the stars above us.
I look at the bowed heads of my friends. It's as
if we're praying or giving a moment's silence
for someone or something we've lost—
which is exactly what we're doing.

Dayspring Christian Academy

A grey box of a school squatting in a dirt lot,
where grass year after year refuses to grow.
Large, glazed wire-meshed windows
allow feeble light for gloom-thick classrooms

where children stammer aloud from gilt-edged bibles.
Dangling above the chalkboard and desks,
a torn Christ listens and watches,
the world's sin in his agonized face.

Pastor Rosio, his face close to mine, rants
about God's great love and our unworthiness.
Spittle dampens my cheeks as I stare into his eyes,
the anger rising in them like the Red Sea's tide

that rose to drown the Egyptians in Jehovah's
wrath. I will not read or speak the page. Cold
as the stone Jesus prayed upon in the garden's
darkness, I take the weight but not the words.

Mr. Steigel

At six feet three inches and two hundred
and fifty pounds, he was a human mountain
when seen through the eyes of a child.
He ran the house that thirteen other boys

and I lived in. His eyes were two grey slits
in a fleshy face gouged with pockmarks.
When he spoke his voice was surprisingly
high and sharp. Because of this,

his nickname among the boys
was the Rat, though no one ever dared
say it in his presence. He hated us,
us being boys from low-income

single-parent families out of Pittsburgh
and Philadelphia. Boys whose mothers
were unable to control them, kicked out
of school after school, with a taste

for petty crimes and vandalism.
Milton Hershey School was the last stop
for me before Shuman Center,
or some other correctional institution.

We woke up every day at 5 A.M.
and did an hour of chores in the dairy barn
before breakfast. After that it was school,
and then back to dorm for more chores,

dinner and study time with an hour
afterwards to watch TV in the common room
before showers and lights out. One night
as I was heading upstairs he called me

through the open door of his office.
Hey, you, get in here! he said
crooking his finger at me. I came
and stood in the doorway.

I was the only boy downstairs.
Come here! he said pointing at a spot
on the carpet beside him. I walked
over as he swivelled his chair

to face me. His doughy forearms
overflowed the armrests they rested on.
His opaque fingernails were thick
and the colour of porridge. I looked

down at his blunt black shoes
and his grey tube socks
showing where his pant legs
had ridden halfway up his shins.

I stared at a lone black hair
curled against the waxy skin
exposed above a sock. *Look
at me!* he said. *I am,* I said.

He came out of the chair
and slammed his knuckles
into my stomach. I hit my head
against the floor as I sucked for air.

He pressed the sole of his shoe
downwards on the side of my face
until I thought my bones
would snap beneath his force.

Mother (Northern British Columbia)

A yard of dust and a glaring sun. A screen door
slaps shut. Gripping a .22 rifle she strides
across the yard to stalk the tractor path

into the fields where she stops to stare.
The sky is a nest of clear flames that burn
above the motionless acres of wheat.

Across the valley, the Peace River
is a giant, blue-dark snake sunning
itself, asleep. Beyond it, the mountains:

enormous, granite-ripped, earthly fleshed
bear shapes that hump sharp-shouldered
the edges of a world her mind

of small farms and sloped green hills can't
contain. Not one head of grain moves
nor cloud floats to break this stillness

that surrounds her. She slips the safety
and grips the trigger, scans the plowed
margins of the field for a flicker of brown.

Gary Powell's Outfitters

A large meadow in the mountains
of British Columbia. At the south end,
the cabin where we lived, and opposite that,
the lodge where the wealthy hunters

stayed. On the western edge, a barn
with stables and a corral where the cowboys
who guided the hunts spent their time.
They tended the horses, but mostly loafed,

slouched against the corral, chewed tobacco,
told stories about their trips into Fort Nelson.
They worked hard in the bush, then off
to town to drink, fuck and fight—free time

spent between the bar, motel and the RCMP
lock-up. My mother called them trash, but my father
wasn't different—a truth she hated to admit,
raising three boys on what pay came home

after his trips to town. The oldest guide, Dan,
his face a cross-hatch of scars and wrinkles,
rode the bulls for ten years when he was young,
and broke more bones, he claimed, than a pretty whore

breaks hearts. One time, he squatted,
grunting at the stiffness in his knees, his face
across from mine, and took out his teeth.
I stared at the glistening pink gums and white teeth

lying in the palm of his huge hand. I saw the nest
of squirming pink-white mice I had found a few days
before behind the lodge. My father came up behind me
and told me to leave them alone, as he tamped

the long, parted grass over the exposed nest.
If the mother smells you she won't come back, she'll
let the babies die. I reached to touch the teeth
in Dan's hand, but he stood up and put them

back in his mouth. *You can take out your own,*
but you've got to find the spot that springs them loose.
And Rod, he added with a wink, *don't touch*
people's teeth. It's not polite. At dinner

that evening in the cabin I couldn't keep
my fingers out of my mouth. I wanted an audience
for my trick. As my mother cleared the table
for dessert my father slapped the side of my head.

Get your hand out of your mouth. What's wrong with you?
He's taking out his teeth! my brother Lynn
volunteered. *What?* My mother turned from the bucket
where she was putting the dirty dishes to look at me.

Do you have a loose tooth? I jabbed my spoon
into the bowl of green Jell-O. *Answer your mother,*
my father said. I told them what Dan
had shown me earlier that day

and why I'd put my fingers in my mouth.
Jell-O sprayed the table as my father
roared. My mother grabbed a cloth and wiped
up the mess, smiling through her teeth.

Heart Lake

It was too small to be a lake.
We lived in a log cabin built by my father
on his trapline next to Williston Lake.
That was my idea of a lake—

ninety-nine miles of shoreline
according to my father, and so wide in places
the opposite shore was a thin dark line
that wavered and blurred the more

you stared. Heart Lake was a pond
you could throw a rock halfway across
and walk around in an hour, which was only
that long because of the brush

that fought your passage along its sides.
We'd come to hunt the black bears
that fed in the dense berry patches
lining the logging road. My father

pulled his battered blue pickup truck
into an empty campsite beside the lake,
and turned the engine off. Behind us the air
was brown with dust that settled

on the leaves of the blackberry bushes
and the hardpacked earth of the road
we'd driven down. The engine ticked
as my father smoked a cigarette. *Is this*

Heart Lake? I asked, disappointed.
Yeah. You don't approve? my father said.
I stayed quiet. The water was the colour
of the dark pines steepling the hills that held it.

It's too small to be a lake, I said. My father
placed the cigarette between his lips,
took a drag and blew the smoke against
the windshield. *But it looks deep, Dad.*

I looked at him. *It's deep enough,* he said,
and heaved the door and left the truck.
Eight years old and scarcely as tall
as the .30-06 slung from his shoulder

by a leather strap, I rushed to keep the pace
he set. The high green walls of vegetation
along the road bristled in the careful silence
my clomping boots and ragged breath

threatened to break. My father stopped,
then held up his hand for me to do the same.
He slid, inch by inch, the rifle
from his shoulder and held it ready

in his hands. I held my breath
and stared to see what he saw. The sunlight
held a weight that etched everything
into the still air, the green tangle

of the blackberry bushes, the dark pines
that stood behind, the dirt and rocks of the road,
the sky hard and blue above us. Then I saw it.
The bushes twitching as a snout emerged,

the lowered head as the huge shoulders
pushed through, and a bear, black as the cast-iron
stove that heated our cabin, stepped into the road.
It stopped, turned, and lifted its head toward us,

its snout searching the air for our smell.
My father, standing straight with the rifle braced
into his shoulder, fired. Thunder tore at my ears
as I pressed my hands against them. The bear

dropped down, faltered as it placed its weight,
then crashed into the dirt. My father held
his hand back up for me to stay where I stood.
The bear began to cough as its sides heaved,

blood swamping its lungs. *It's almost a human
sound,* my father said to himself
as we watched. The bear finally gone still,
my father stepped toward it, his rifle raised.

Get! Get! he shouted and stopped,
but the bear stayed still. He bent to pick up
a rock and bounced it, with a throw,
against its side. The bear lay motionless

and made no sound. My father waved me
forward until we stood above it. *I'll go back
to the lake and get the truck*, he said. *You
stay here and guard the bear.* He hung

the rifle from his shoulder and left. I went
to the side of the road and found a stick.
I circled the bear and lightly poked
the padded paws and claws

lying harmless now in the dust. I poked
the matted fur and gagged at the musky scent
that stung my nose. Already, flies
were gathering about its head and clinging

to the nostrils caked with blood. I stomped
and waved them off, then pushed apart
the black lips to bare the yellow incisors
that frightened me even with the thing dead.

The bear's head lolled as its body
shifted and the jaws caught at my stick.
I jumped back and fell against the ground,
then lifted myself partway up, my arms

shaking, palms pressed into the dirt,
to watch the bear as I had been told to. Scared,
I didn't hear the truck pull up or my father
slam the door as he got out. *It's a dead*

bear, Rod. It just looks alive, he said,
and laughed. I saw his dusty cowboy boots
next to my hand. I looked up the whole length
of his body, the sun directly behind his head,

the light streaming through his hair
like strands of fire around his face. *Is the bear
big enough for you?* he asked. *Yes*,
I said and shut my eyes against the glare.

Trumpeter Swan

On an evening in early September,
when the clouds against the dimming sun
were the colour of dark honey,
my mother shot a .22-calibre shell

through the outstretched neck
of what she claimed she'd thought
was a Canada Goose as it flew
above the wheat field behind the barn.

A difficult shot she loved to brag about
to my father's friends when they
came by the house to drink with him—
until Gary the Newfie, part-time bartender

at the Hudson's Hope Hotel, his chair
tilted back against the kitchen wall,
a cigarette in one hand and a beer
in the other, said, *You'd think anyone*

with such a good eye would easily
know the difference between a common goose
and a protected bird, especially one
that carries a two-thousand-dollar fine.

My father chuckled and smacked
my mother's ass as she stalked
past the table and out to the porch
to sit and smoke in the darkness.

The Hunting Knife

I keep my father's hunting knife on my desk.
I set it there the day it arrived wrapped
in a narrow parcel that sat in my hand
like a small coffin. I unwrapped it

with some care—there might've been a letter
inside I didn't wish to tear—but there
was only the knife, the blade folded
within the black handle. I'd held this knife

when I was thirteen gutting my first
deer as he gave instructions,
his voice the edge that slit the white belly.
This was a serious business—

his knowledge passed on. His hand
on my back, the scooped guts steaming
in the snow. We carried the slack corpse
out of the woods and set it in the bed

of the truck parked just off the road. My father
slammed the tailgate shut and walked
toward the cab. *Good thing it didn't snow,*
was all he said on the long drive home.

The Lightning Catcher

On a Friday evening in deep summer
my father has come home from the tavern,
and sits in the kitchen in his work clothes.
Cigarette burning in one dirt-hardened hand,
with the other he grabs me by the arm,
laughs as the coal dust makes me sneeze,
says, *You can catch lightning in your*
hands if you're quick enough, pushes
me away and reaches back for his beer.

The flicker of fireflies in the air dims
and the alley is dark except for the weak
street-lamp light outside Cooper's Tire Garage.
I let a mayonnaise jar drop from my hand.
It shatters against concrete, my captive
dying fireflies crawling out over the glass.
I hear beginnings of thunder and climb
the fire escape that hangs down from the side
of our apartment building, go to the tar roof.

The Allegheny River curves dark green
below me. Car headlights move along
Pittsburgh Street. Beneath railyard lights
the train tracks run black through the glare
of white gravel, and the steel bridges
more numerous than I had imagined
connect darkness with darkness
as I stand scabby-kneed on the roof,
surveying what is suddenly my kingdom.

Thunder pounds like detonating shells,
stripping the air. When the lightning hits,
it blinds me, clouds slide behind my eyes.
I could be crawling over the tar, sharp rain
falling around me, or standing in darkness
above the house, shaking. I feel someone
moving behind me. I know the smell
of tobacco, sweat, beer and coal dust.
I'm quick enough to know it's my father.

Mining for Gold

We built the sluice boxes in the living room
of our apartment on 72 Avenue in Surrey.
We worked in the evenings while Margaret,
my stepmother, tended bar at the Newton Inn

on King George Highway. As we measured,
cut and assembled the pieces of wood,
my father told me how the process worked.
The bottoms would be lined with carpet

laid beneath iron mesh and angled
at a downward slope, a one-inch drop
per foot of length, to catch the gold
as water rushed the lighter soil

through—the flake settling within the carpet,
the nuggets lodging within the mesh. He'd
rented a small backhoe in Quesnel.
We'd use it to dig through the topsoil

until we reached bedrock. Then we'd
find the real deposits and strike it rich.
*The Cariboo is not mined out, there's lots
of gold left up there. One day someone's*

*gonna find a huge seam. You never know,
it could be us.* Topographical maps
and diagrams for various mining schemes
were spread across the dinner table.

He'd stay up half the night, studying them
through a cloud of cigarette smoke.
In the mornings he'd pound on my bedroom
door to hand me a cup of coffee. As I

got ready for school he'd tell me stories
about Billy Barker, John "Cariboo" Cameron
and his wife Sophie who died just before he
struck it rich, and the Hanging Judge,

Matthew Begbie, who, according to my father
hanged over thirty men. *It was a tough place,
Rod. Hangings were necessary. You'd
be surprised at the things men*

will do if there's no law around.
On the morning we left to go north,
he made us a small breakfast. *We'll
stop for a big meal at Hell's Gate,*

he said, and slapped my shoulder
so hard I nearly dropped my plate
of scrambled eggs as I headed
for the table. *What's Hell's Gate,*

Dad? I asked as Margaret sipped
her coffee, chuckled, and shook her head.
*It's the gateway to the Cariboo, Rod,
and all the gold that we can dig.*

Pink Mountain

My father called it Pink Mountain,
which made me think of bubble gum—
but that's what everyone called it.
Pink Mountain. A two-hour drive

outside Fort St. John, a town of Indians
and cowboys in from reserves and oil fields
to party for the weekend, fights
in the streets as they staggered

between the Condill Hotel
and the Ford Motor Inn. Men who knew
the backcountry and knew my father,
the bouncer at the Condill Hotel.

I'd listen late at night, pretend
to be asleep when he'd stagger in
and bend down to kiss my forehead.
I'd listen to the drunken stories he'd tell

my mother. A broken pool cue
over the back of Tarzan, the Native trapper
who came into town on his dogsled.
Dogs snarling in the traces, gnarled hands,

big hunting knife dangling
from his belt, the knife he cut men with—
but my father took him. Threw him out
the door into the street. Everyone

talked about it for weeks. There were stories
about the war. My father's voice
slurred and hard. My mother saying,
It's alright honey, let's get some sleep.

He'd stay up talking to himself,
the sound of the bottle against the glass,
until he passed out. Once I heard him
cry, deep sobs shaking me in my bed.

And on one other occasion, the night
he held me in his lap, I watched blankly
as his eyes grew wet. Perched like a sparrow
on the bone of his knee, the goat's head

hanging from the trailer wall across from me,
I was a witness to the truth—he wasn't
really my father. My mother coughing
as she rose from the couch to leave the room.

The next day was the last time I saw him
for years. He loaded the car for a hunting trip
to Pink Mountain. He kissed me on the forehead,
said he'd back Monday morning.

Mrs. Tobin

She ran a boarding house on Doman Street
in South Vancouver. The boarders, all men,
lived in the basement, two to a room. My father
had moved up north and I'd come to the city

alone on a bus from Cranbrook.
I found her ad in the classifieds and took
a cab straight from the station to her house.
I had enough money to cover the first month's

rent and moved in that afternoon
with my belongings stuffed in a bag.
She was a large woman with a red face
and dyed hair. Her husband had been

a master sergeant, but died a year
after he retired. When she asked my age
I told her I was twenty-one, but she
laughed and said, *Don't lie to me honey*

or you can find somewhere else to live.
So I told her the truth, that my dad
had left me to go up north and I'd
quit school to come to the city

to live on my own. The next day
she took me to the welfare office
and argued with a case worker
and a supervisor until they

agreed to pay my room and board
if I went back to school. Mount Baker
had been a semester school
and there were two in the Lower Mainland.

Mrs. Tobin took me to them both that day.
Magee was for the city's rich kids
and turned me away, but New West Secondary
said I could start classes the next morning.

That evening, my new roommate Ken
took me to the Cobalt to watch strippers
and to have some beers. Before we
left the house he showed me a baseball

card, perfectly preserved, from 1967.
It featured a young Ken, in a Detroit Tigers
uniform standing on the dugout steps
with a bat resting on his shoulder, a huge grin

spread across his broad face. *I played*
two seasons until I broke my back
in a motorcycle accident. I couldn't play
after that. I've got arthritis now.

It hurts all the time. But fuck it
eh? I'm lucky to be alive, so ain't no point
in bitching. Ken was on disability
and three or four times a year

got paid to carry cocaine in a backpack
via bus to Montreal or Toronto. He
had a gambling problem and spent
his meagre winnings on prostitutes,

but Mrs. Tobin liked him and he
always paid his rent. At the bar Ken
walked me past the bouncers
who nodded their heads as we

passed. He called a waitress by name
and ordered a pitcher of draft. When she
left he said, *I got you in, so you can buy the drinks.*
Okay? I nodded my head and paid

the waitress when she returned. Three hours
later I was throwing up in a urinal. A man
shoved me as I swayed toward the sinks
to wash my face. I slipped and fell

against the filthy tiles sleek with piss
and water. I got up and puked again into a sink.
At the table Ken was gone and so were
our drinks. I sat down and watched

the stripper. A power ballad
began to blare through the speakers.
She was nude and her breasts
hung and gleamed with sweat

as she bent over to pick up a folded quilt
at the edge of the stage. She flung it
outwards and dropped it open on the floor.
She walked a slow circle around it,

grinding her hips. I was drawn
to the perfect blankness of her face.
I stood up and walked toward
the stage. I felt I was the only person

there besides her. The singer's voice
peaked at the chorus of the song, but no words
were being sung, there were only sounds
that moved across her like the stage lights

that pulsed and crisscrossed against her
body. She laid her belly against the quilt,
and began to grind her hips into the floor.
Her hand flickered between her legs

like a small trapped bird as she
mocked playing with herself. On her
left ankle I saw a blue tattoo of a heart
with wings. I reached out to touch it.

Her body whipped away from me
the instant my fingers touched her skin.
I saw a garter snake I had tapped
lightly with a stick behind my uncle's barn.

It shivered then flashed into a hole
beneath the faded boards of the wall.
She was standing, her dark hair
wild against her face. She was

pointing at me. I looked at her eyes
and she screamed *Don't touch me*
you fucking freak! You don't touch
the fucking dancers! Get the fuck

out of here! A deep warm voice
spoke into my ear, it made me
think of the murky water we
would dive into off the banks

of the river. *Okay, buddy, it's time*
to go. Come on. A hand gripped
my arm just above the elbow
and guided me between the tables

toward the bouncer at the front door.
He pushed it open and pushed me
through it onto the sidewalk.
Go home pal, you're covered

in puke, he said and pulled the door
shut. The air was a thin drizzle
of rain against my face, headlights
slid like the blurred tails of comets

through the dark. I reached
into my pockets but they were empty.
I lowered my head and stepped
off the edge of the world.

Fight

He'd been stealing my letters from the front desk.
The woman who cleaned the rooms found them
when she emptied the garbage from his room.
He'd written all over them in red ink

slut, whore, cunt. I didn't know why he did it.
I was seventeen and living in the Tudor House
Hotel in Cranbrook. He and I would snort
coke together in my room so we could drink

all night. Sometimes men shouted in the hallway,
kicked a body down the stairs, we'd do a line,
turn the radio up and pretend not to hear.
I didn't know why he did it and I didn't care

to know. She'd been sick for months
and wasn't going to get better. He knew
what the letters meant to me. I went into the bar
and asked if he wanted to smoke a joint.

It was January and the parking lot was ice
and hardpacked snow. When he took the joint
and put it in his mouth I hit him as hard
as I could. His head snapped, the joint

flew and he went down. I rushed to kick him,
but he didn't try to get up. He curled into a ball
and covered his face with his arms. I screamed
Get up and fight! but he just lay there. It was quiet

and I could hear the low buzz of the streetlight.
It sounded like a woman humming a song to herself.
That's when the crying started. I kicked him
but he wouldn't get back up and fight.

Everywhere You Look

You wake from a dream and stare
into the blackness of the room.
The window behind your head is open.
A breeze, soft as hair, comes in
through the curtains and touches

your chest. You remember her hair.
A single strand was like the touch
of fire against your skin. Is there a way
to talk about this without seeming
absurd? Her face in the dream is hard,

as if she is wearing a mask. As if
the years of your life have been
pressed into the image of the face
that stares at you from across a table.
It is mid-afternoon. The sunlight

over the tables and the traffic
and the white awning that reminds
you of a great, solitary wing anointed
with oil is heavy with a silence you wish
to touch, but always refuses you.

She watches her finger drawing
an invisible sign on the tablecloth.
Everywhere you look are signs you
cannot read. It has always been
this way, from the waiter who shifts

his eyes away from yours, to the filthy river
that sang to you more than any prayer
you were forced to utter to a god you hated,
to your mother's screams and your father's
drunkenness. She lifts her eyes across

your forty-two years to meet your gaze.
She is the river, the snow fields, the neon
in the rain. She is everything that has been
taken from you and never returned. You lie
in a room that she has never left and never will.

My Father's Watch

I fasten my father's watch around my wrist.
It dangles at the end of my arm like an oversized
bracelet. I don't adjust the clasp to make it fit.
I want to wear it as my father wore it.

I watched him once when we moved homes.
I marvelled at his strength. He lifted boxes
two times larger than me. I'm a child
dressed up in my father's clothes.

We hadn't talked for three years. Then cancer
grew tumours in his stomach. He'd call me
after chemotherapy. *I'm tired,* he'd say.
I've got to rest for a while.

It was pneumonia that killed him. He was right.
The cancer wouldn't claim him. The night
before he died he told me to stop worrying.
Don't turn this into a soap opera, he said.

I knew this was our last chance to talk but did as he said,
hung up the phone. I went to bed and slept.
Twelve people stood around him until the morning.
They prayed and sang his favourite songs.

His eyes are blank as water. The hand
that lifted lies battered on the sheet. The green
band too large on his thin wrist would remind me
of spring, but I won't see him again.

IV

Starlings

Even on this quiet Sunday morning,
the starlings make constant argument.
Scrawny and fierce, they fight each other
for the bird seed that darkens the snow
like a spray of shotgun pellets.

The lawn is a prison cell, black bars
of shadow laid down by rippling arms
of trees against the snow. But the starlings
know no limits, they move from ground
to air, through black and white, as easily

as they send out a tirade of chirps, whistles,
squawks and clicks. Bird-curses flow up
and down musical scales as effortlessly as
the winds they travel. Oddly speckled birds,
without grace, their black sheathed within a sheen

of green, they are a mock-storm of sound
and darkness against this winter's cold
that makes me stop until my fingers go numb.
I drop the trash into the can. They rise in one
startled wave to quarrel among the trees.

Willy Soble

My brother Lynn is sitting beside me
on a park bench in Hamilton. I
don't know the name of the park
or what part of the city we're

in as I'm passing through
to play a show someplace else.
I haven't seen my brother
in nearly fifteen years. We

talk about the neighbourhood
we grew up in and the people
we knew. Lynn tells me the news
about our friend Willy Soble

and his father who raised pit bulls
in the backyard for dog fights
when we were kids. He says
they kidnapped, raped and threatened

to kill a young girl, but she escaped
when they got drunk and forgot
to tie her up again. They're doing twenty years
at the state prison in Somerset, Pennsylvania.

A year after they were sentenced, the girl
committed suicide. I remember Willy,
a skinny kid with Scotch-taped glasses
who hardly spoke, and when he did you

could barely hear him. I remember
the dark bruises on his arms
and face and the day I found him
sitting against the garage in the alley

unable to stop shaking. I remember
the way his father beat and kicked
the dogs in the backyard and how
he punched his wife and knocked her

down the back-porch steps for asking him
to stop. I remember Willy laughing
behind Podmilsak's Grocery
early one evening as we

split a pack of stolen cigarettes,
and the way I felt watching his eyes
fill up with something other than silence,
and something other than fear.

I was unable to understand what I saw,
unable to tell him this momentary, laughing self
was the part of him they could never have,

but I was wrong and so was Willy.

The Ride

He picked me up on the Trans-Canada
Highway, just east of Medicine Hat.
The car, an old Buick sedan,
stank of dog hair and cigarette smoke.

An open case of Molson Canadian
was sitting on the front seat next to him.
A German shepherd lay the length
of the back seat. As I got into the car,

it raised its head, growled, then flopped
back down and closed its eyes. *Where
you headed? I don't know, Montreal
I guess. Well, I'm going to Regina.*

*That'll work for now. You
don't have any stuff? No, I lost
my backpack in Calgary. Sounds
like a hell of a night! Yeah, you*

*could put it that way. A young guy's
got to have a good time. What's your name?
Rodney. Rodney, grab yourself a beer
and I'll grab the wheel.* He was drunk,

but it was January and the winds
whipping across the prairies
drove the cold so hard into my body
I was shaking and couldn't stop.

That's a hell of a shiner you got.
I don't want to talk about it,
if you don't mind. Suit yourself, son.
I took a warm beer out of the case

and popped the cap off with my lighter,
took a drink and shut my eyes.
Grateful for the dog hair,
stench of old cigarette smoke,

warm beer and the ride in a car
through a landscape intent,
it seemed, on killing me, I leaned
back into the seat and fell asleep.

When I awoke he was beating the palm
of one hand against the steering wheel,
wildly keeping time with the song
in his head, that only he could hear.

The Song That Says

Junkies scatter like frightened crabs
as I walk down Union Street past the park
smeared with goose shit. Seagulls flash
white crosses above the Chinatown rooftops,
screaming as they dive to fight for food.

Merchants in white aprons delicately place
fish on ice graves like rows of detached,
silver tongues, as delivery boys shout
over the rattle-clank of cars and trucks.
In the midst of this a young man stands,

his stiff clothes stinking of urine and shit.
A woman makes an involuntary retching
sound as she drops a coin into his bloated,
bruised hand. He rocks on feet wrapped
in canvas and moans a long howl

like that of a dog I found once in Oaxaca,
its hindquarters crushed, tossed into a ditch
to die. The same howl broke from me
in a Montreal tenement, the empty sockets
of a child's face staring through the frozen

window mirroring my own blackness. The young
man's howl and my own the same as that of a drunk
or a broken animal or a child who has been raped.
It is the song we will not hear. The song
that says our pain is too ugly to look upon.

Home

The rustle of plastic bags
outside my door tells me
my neighbour has returned home.
I listen for the muted chime

of keys pulled from the pocket
and raised to the lock, the thud
of the turned bolt and the slam
of the door pulled shut against

its frame. I know my neighbour
teaches at a local college and often,
at night, sings drunkenly to himself.
When we pass in the hallway

we nod but seldom speak. Once,
I heard him shouting outside
the Latin Quarter on a Friday night.
A man walked up and knocked him

down with a single punch. I
watched my neighbour clutch
at a pole to get to his feet, sway,
steady himself, then lurch away

onto the grass of Grandview Park
and into the darkness like a wobbling
planet flung from its orbit. I felt
for my keys and went home.

The Trumpet

A man blows from a trumpet a high, bright note.
He's come to play the sound of April sunlight
filling Grandview Park, the sound of cherry blossoms
so ethereal they might burst into small, fiery clouds,
to play the strange affection one suddenly feels for one's
neighbours in this ambivalent, rain-sodden city.

Small children tumble from swings and a jungle gym
to waddle toward him. A ring of small trumpeters
forms to pay tribute. He's an emissary of the sun
come to herald the spring. They know it, but he
doesn't. He simply wishes to be free of his narrow,
humid room above the Uprising Bakery.

He plays a silver sound, like the long strand of saliva
streaming from a young man's mouth as his head
sags, and he dreams the gleaming sweep of a curve
in the Bow River, where he and his brothers fished
for trout, before the sun charred the sky to blackness
and the river and the fish and everyone got drunk.

A man blows from a trumpet a high, bright note.
We stand inside it as we stand inside this sunlight
flooding the parks and streets and alleys of the city,
this light that pulls the bright blades from the browned
earth, as thousands of small, forgotten deaths rise up, grateful
for the spring and this light that leaves only to return.

What Is Ours

I'm drinking espresso outside Joe's Cafe
on an evening in early spring. A brown cup
sits on a small, white tabletop at my left.
The cup is empty but for the remains

of espresso and sugar pooled at the bottom.
The air is cool against my hands and face,
and rich with the scent of cherry blossoms
clogging the gutters of Commercial Drive.

Soon I'll get up and walk back
to my apartment on Charles Street
where I've lived alone for several years.
I'll take out my keys and twirl them

on my finger as I approach the door
to the building. I'll pause, after sliding
the key into the lock, to look back
at the mountains becoming night.

Days Like This

We stand inside a doorway to share
a cigarette. The rain comes straight
down: long strands of blown glass
shattering against the concrete.

I tell you this, how the rain appears
to me, and you say no, the street is a face
and the drops are not shards of shattering
glass but tears from a blind god's eyes.

In this darkness I can almost not see
the sores on your face, how your hand
shakes as you lift the cigarette to your lips,
how your eyes shatter with each glance.

You tell me about the landlord who stole
your cheque and threw you out of your room,
how I must believe you, as I watch
you looking for someone to silence

the rat tearing at your stomach, to calm
your fingers picking at the scabs on your skin,
the blood crusted under your eaten nails.
You will die on this street in the rain,

or in a doorway or half-naked in an alley.
You hand the cigarette back to me and our
fingers touch. You smile and for a moment
we are walking through the rain-mist

and pink petals of cherry blossoms.
You take my arm and pull me to you.
You tell me that days like this are proof
we live forever. I smell the spring rain

damp in your hair. Your breath leaves you
as easily as the rain falls to the street
to shatter like broken glass. Days like this
are proof of what we will have to lose.

Behind the Gasworks on Railroad Avenue

Where white storage tanks sit in gravel and tar,
my brother and I push our bicycles
into a vacant lot of dust and far-apart trees
that throw skinny shade against a white

one-storey brick and concrete building
that was once a factory. We lay
our bicycles on the ground and sit
with our backs against the coolness

of the brick wall. Our legs thrust out
before us in the dust. It doesn't matter
that we are wearing cut-offs and our legs
will be stained with the dust and our sweat.

We are too young to separate ourselves
from the day with its load of sunlight
and dirt. We are tired and do not talk.
We turn the dirt through our fingers

and my brother says, *Look*, and holds
his hand out to me. Two pieces of pig iron
in his dirt-smeared palm. *They're
as black as crow feathers*, I say. He puts

them in his pocket. Says quietly,
*Crow feathers, boy that's a
good one*. We sit a while longer.
I notice our breath rising and falling

and how effortless it seems. This
is the summer day that comes back to me
when my brother I haven't heard from
in a year or two calls tonight

to say he is living in Jacksonville
in a treatment centre and no liquor
has passed his lips for three weeks.
His ex-wife, who won't speak his name,

will let him see his son if he stays sober
for a year. He still has the two pieces
of pig iron wrapped in cloth in a drawer.
He says they help him to stay sober

and do I remember that day and how
I said crow feathers. I see the white storage
tanks, barbed wire, gravel and tar.
Yes, I say, and set the phone softly down.

Ruins

Sitting at his desk he stares at the printout
thumbtacked to the wall. The building
in the photograph sags as if about to collapse.

The brick façade, once painted white,
is blackened from traffic exhaust. Swollen tar
shingles curl and peel away from the awning

above the shop windows. Alongside the building
runs the shattered alley leading to the garage
and the apartment above. The stuccoed walls

are cracked and water-stained. Sheets of plywood,
nailed up and painted-over, patch the spots
where chunks of plaster have given way.

The once-bright red letters of the Cooper's
Tire sign are a smeared and washed-out pink.
He leans back in his seat and shuts his eyes.

Weeds take over the alley's broken asphalt,
spring's advance troops reclaiming ground,
and across the road, engorged with melted snow,

the Allegheny surges toward Pittsburgh's trinity
of waters as fireflies slowly begin to spark
the darkening air like small brief stars.

Certain Things

You want me to say things I can't.
You want me to say the full moon
over Pachek's garage on summer
evenings meant nothing to me. Or I
didn't notice the smell of damp grass

or the cooing of pigeons in the mornings
when I awoke. The sound of my brother's
muted trumpet one Saturday didn't make
my eyes fill with tears for reasons I still
can't explain. I didn't break my best friend's

nose outside Shoop's restaurant one night
and then kick him in the back after he fell
on the ice. I don't remember thinking
the blood on the snow was like ketchup
on an off-white tablecloth, or that later he

apologized to me while I stared at my feet.
I didn't once stand on the #16
Highway in Alberta in January, my own
nose broken, hitching I didn't know where
except farther away. Twenty years later,

in Vancouver at 2:00 A.M., my brother
doesn't call to tell me he's got cancer
and *It's too soon*, neither of us with any idea
where we're going. It isn't all I or anyone
can do, but try to see where we've been.

Marked

The July dusk light burns
above the slow push of the current.
The green tangle of woods
and the low-slung Appalachian hills

rise on the opposite shore
close to where you stand.
You could walk the dark slate
of the river then disappear

into the clutching shadows
of those hills, but the sky
darkens slowly and you
wait here at the edge of water.

On your left a ruined barge
protrudes from the river,
an enormous, broken wing.
Grey-rubbled piles of pig iron

lie alongside the rusted tracks
mirroring the river's course.
Dust off the burnt ground
marks your hands, bare legs

and shoes. A robin darts,
blood-orange, among the willows.
You see you are the memory
the river becomes in you.

Acknowledgements

I'd like to acknowledge Russell Thornton for helping me to become a better poet, William and Matilda Ferguson (my grandpa and grandma who both died while I was writing the book), Lynn DeCroo, Chris Decroo (my brothers), Al Mader and Brad Yaksich.

About the Author

Rodney DeCroo is a Vancouver-based singer/songwriter and poet. Born and raised in a small coal-mining town just outside of Pittsburgh, Pennsylvania, he has called Vancouver home for twenty years now. He has released five CDs that have received critical acclaim in Canada, the United States and Europe. Music critics have called him one of Canada's best folk/alt-country songwriters.